Taking Asthma to School

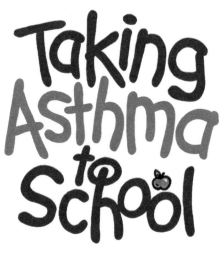

by

Kim Gosselin

JayJo Books, LLC.
Publishing Special Books for Special Kids®

Taking Asthma to School
Copyright © 1998 by Kim Gosselin
Edited by Barbara A. Mitchell
No part of this book may be reproduced or transmitted in any form or by any means, electronic or mechanical, including photocopying, recording, or by any information storage and retrieval system without written permission from the publisher. All rights reserved. Printed in the United States of America.

Published by
JayJo Books, LLC
A Guidance Channel Company
Publishing Special Books for Special Kids®

JayJo Books is a publisher of books to help teachers, parents, and children cope with chronic illnesses, special needs, and health education in classroom, family, and social settings.

Library of Congress Cataloging-in-Publication Data
Gosselin, Kim
Taking Asthma to School/Kim Gosselin
Second Edition-Third Printing/Revised
Library of Congress Control Number 97-76662
1. Juvenile/Non-Fiction   2. Asthma   3. Education

ISBN 1-891383-01-9
Second book in our *Special Kids in School®* series

NOTE:
The opinions expressed in **Taking Asthma to School** are those solely of the author. Asthma care is highly individualized. One should **never** alter asthma care without first consulting a member of the individual's professional asthma medical team.

For information about Premium and Special Sales, contact:
JayJo Books Special Sales Office
P.O. Box 213
Valley Park, MO 63088-0213
636-861-1331
jayjobooks@aol.com

For all other information, contact:
JayJo Books
A Guidance Channel Company
135 Dupont Street, P.O. Box 760
Plainview, NY 11803-0760
1-800-999-6884
jayjobooks@guidancechannel.com
www.jayjo.com

ABOUT THE AUTHOR

Kim Gosselin was born and raised in Michigan where she attended Central Michigan University. She began her professional writing career shortly after her two young sons were both diagnosed with chronic illnesses. Kim is extremely committed to bringing the young reader quality children's health education while raising important funds for medical research.

Kim now resides and writes in Missouri. She is an avid supporter of the Epilepsy Foundation of America, the American Lung Association, the American Cancer Society, and a member of the American Diabetes Association, the Juvenile Diabetes Foundation International, the Society of Children's Book Writers and Illustrators, the Small Publishers Association of North America, the Publishers Marketing Association, and The Author's Guild.

Kim received the 1998 President's Award from the National Office of the American Lung Association for her work with chronically ill children and the 1998 National Female Family Friendly Business Award.

Hello boys and girls! My name is Justin, and I'm a kid living with asthma. Having asthma means part of my body called the lungs and bronchial tubes don't always work the way they are supposed to. Because of this, it's hard for me to breathe sometimes.

Everyone has lungs and bronchial tubes, but not everyone gets asthma.

Doctors and nurses don't know why I have asthma. I didn't do anything wrong, and it's **nobody's** fault! Doctors and nurses do know you can't catch asthma from me. It's okay to play with me and be my friend.

I can't give you asthma.

Sometimes having asthma makes it hard for me to breathe. This is called an asthma "episode." To help prevent an asthma episode, it helps if I use my inhaler that has special medicine in it. Usually I use something called a "spacer" with my inhaler. Spacers come in different shapes and sizes, but they all help get the medicine deep into my lungs (where it works best).

Using my inhaler and spacer doesn't hurt, and it isn't scary either! I breathe in big puffs of medicine, and then my breathing is just right!

Because I have asthma, it's important to pay close attention to things that may "trigger" an asthma episode. Like me, many kids with asthma have allergies too! Allergies can trigger asthma, so I try to stay away from things I'm allergic to. Some of these things might be dust, pollen, smoke, mold, or animals with fur or feathers.

It can help my asthma if I stay away from things that I'm allergic to.

To help keep my asthma in good control, I have a special tool that measures how much air is in my lungs. This is called a peak-flow meter. I take in a big breath and blow air into the meter. If the air in my lungs measures too low, it's probably best for me to use my inhaler. I always write down my peak-flow measurements in a little book. This helps my doctors and nurses decide how much medicine I need.

Sometimes my peak-flow meter tells me an asthma episode is coming. If I use my inhaler, I might even be able to prevent it!

When I do have an asthma episode, I might act differently than I normally do. Breathing in and out sometimes gets very hard. I might start to cough or choke. My chest may feel tight and my skin might turn pale or get sweaty. At times my breathing makes wheezing or whistling sounds. Please tell the teacher if you see me act this way. I need to use my rescue inhaler **fast** when I'm having an asthma episode. A rescue inhaler may help to stop an asthma episode.

After a few minutes, I'm usually back to my old self again!

Like most kids, I love to play at recess and take part in gym class. I bet you do too! Because exercise usually triggers an asthma episode for me (and for many other kids too), it's probably best for me to use my peak-flow meter and inhaler before doing lots of exercise. Then I'm sure to have plenty of energy to play and have fun.

As long as I keep my asthma in good control, it doesn't stop me from doing **anything** other kids do!

Maybe someday there will be a cure for asthma. That means my doctors and nurses will be able to stop it. Until then, please don't treat me any differently just because I have asthma.

After all, nobody's perfect. In fact, I bet I'm a lot like you in every other way!

Peak-flow book

DIFFERENT KINDS
OF SPACERS

INHALERS

PEAK-FLOW
METERS

lungs
+
bronchial tubes

THE END

STAR SHIP

LET'S TAKE THE ASTHMA KIDS' QUIZ!

1. What part of my body is affected by asthma?
   My lungs and bronchial tubes.

2. Can you catch asthma from me or anybody else?
   No, asthma is not contagious!

3. Did I do anything wrong to cause my asthma?
   No, and it's nobody's fault either!

Pollen

4. What does having asthma make it hard for me to do sometimes?
   Breathe.

5. What is it called when it becomes hard for me to breathe in or out?
   An asthma "episode."

6. What are some of the signs of an asthma episode?
   Coughing, choking, pale or sweaty skin, wheezing or whistling sounds when I breathe.

Dust

7. Does having asthma stop me from doing anything other kids do?
   No, as long as I keep my asthma in good control, I can do anything you can do!

   Great job! Thanks for taking the Asthma Kids' Quiz!

Animal Fur

Ten Tips For Teachers

1. **WHEN A CHILD HAS ASTHMA, HIS (OR HER) BRONCHIAL TUBES AND LUNGS DON'T ALWAYS WORK THE WAY THEY ARE SUPPOSED TO.** This makes it hard for them to breathe sometimes and they should always be checked by the school nurse if they are having trouble breathing.

2. **THE PARTS OF THE BODY THAT ARE AFFECTED IN A CHILD LIVING WITH ASTHMA ARE THE BRONCHIAL TUBES AND THE LUNGS.** You may hear a wheezing or "whistling" sound coming from the child when they breathe in or out, or they may have choking or coughing spells while trying to breathe. They should be seen by the nurse and use the correct, prescribed medication right away!

3. **DON'T TREAT A CHILD LIVING WITH ASTHMA AS HAVING A SIMPLE CONDITION.** Many things affect a child's asthma including emotions, pollution, allergies, environment (both at home and school), pets in the classroom and exercise, among others. Try to pay attention to your student's specific asthma "triggers," and remove them from the classroom whenever possible.

4. **IF POSSIBLE, LET THE CHILD LIVING WITH ASTHMA HAVE EASY ACCESS TO HIS OR HER INHALER.** My son's teacher allows it to be placed in a special "teachers" drawer, where he can retrieve it whenever necessary (according to his doctor's directions, of course!) Sometimes using it in class (if needed) can easily prevent a trip to the nurse which isn't always convenient or necessary. This should only be allowed with the doctor's, principal's, and parent's permission, of course. And remember, some schools don't even have a school nurse, so medications are left to the responsibility of the school secretary or someone with even less medical training.

5. **MAKE SURE THE CHILD LIVING WITH ASTHMA AND HIS CLASSMATES UNDERSTAND THAT ASTHMA IS NOT CONTAGIOUS!**
    Although approximately 1 in 15 children have asthma, there are many factors contributing to the condition. Being contagious is not one of them.

6. **SOME VERY SMALL CHILDREN MAY NEED TO USE A "SPACER" OR A NEBULIZER WITH THEIR ASTHMA MEDICATION.**
    This probably should be done in the nurse's office and helps the medicine get deep into their lungs, where it works best!

7. **NEVER REFER TO THE CHILD LIVING WITH ASTHMA AS THE "ASTHMATIC KID," ETC.**
    This often happens in gym class when a student is living with exercise-induced asthma (please refer to the book **SPORTSercise!** for more information on this topic). Kids living with asthma are no different than other children, they just have to incorporate asthma episodes into their lives and take certain precautions. Remember, asthma is just a very small part of who they are!

8. **IT ALWAYS HELPS FOR THE STUDENT LIVING WITH ASTHMA TO HAVE HIS OR HER OWN "PEAK-FLOW" METER IN THE NURSE'S OFFICE (IF AVAILABLE).**
    This way the child who has an asthma episode can actually measure the amount of air coming out of his or her lungs. This tells the nurse how serious the student's asthma episode is and when their parents or doctor should be notified.

9. **REMEMBER, A CHILD WHO HAS BEEN SICK WITH ASTHMA OR HAS RECENTLY HAD AN ASTHMA EPISODE MAY NEED A LITTLE EXTRA TIME TO CATCH UP.**
    They probably won't feel very well for a while after an asthma episode and may have difficulty in concentrating. Be sensitive to their situation and allow them a little extra time if at all possible.

10. **A CHILD WITH ASTHMA IS NO DIFFERENT THAN ANY OTHER STUDENT IN YOUR CLASSROOM.**
    Allow them to grow at their own pace and demonstrate their individuality just as you would with any other student.

To order additional copies of *Taking Asthma To School* or inquire about our quantity discounts for schools, hospitals, and affiliated organizations, contact us at 1-800-999-6884.

From our *Special Kids in School*® series
Taking A.D.D. to School
Taking Cerebral Palsy to School
Taking Cystic Fibrosis to School
Taking Diabetes to School
Taking Food Allergies to School
Taking Seizure Disorders to School
...and others coming soon!

From our new *Healthy Habits for Kids*™ series:
There's a Louse in My House
A Fun Story about Kids and Head Lice
...and others coming soon!

Other books available now!
SPORTSercise!
A School Story about
Exercise-Induced Asthma
ZooAllergy
A Fun Story about Allergy
and Asthma Triggers
Rufus Comes Home
Rufus The Bear With Diabetes™
A Story About Diagnosis and Acceptance
The ABC's of Asthma
An Asthma Alphabet Book
for Kids of All Ages
Taming the Diabetes Dragon
A Story about Living Better
with Diabetes

Trick or Treat for Diabetes
A Halloween Story for Kids Living with Diabetes

And from our *Substance Free Kids*® series
Smoking STINKS!!™

A portion of the proceeds from all our publications is donated to various charities to help fund important medical research and education. We work hard to make a difference in the lives of children with chronic conditions and/or special needs. Thank you for your support.